KSS VELOCETTE

Jeff Clew

FOREWORD	4
HISTORY	5
EVOLUTION	10
SPECIFICATION	13
ROAD TESTS	15
OWNERS' VIEW	20
BUYING	23
CLUBS, SPECIALISTS & BOOKS	25
PHOTO GALLERY	26

ISBN 0 85429 444 9

A FOULIS Motorcycling Book

First published 1984

© Haynes Publishing Group

All rights reserved. No part of this book may be reproduced or transmitted in any form or by any means, electronic or mechanical, including photocopying, recording or by any information storage or retrieval system, without written permission from the publisher.

Published by:
Haynes Publishing Group
Sparkford, Yeovil,
Somerset BA22 7JJ

Distributed in USA by:
Haynes Publications Inc.
861 Lawrence Drive, Newbury Park, California 91320, USA

British Library Cataloguing in Publication Data

Clew, Jeff
 Velocette KSS Super Profile.
 -(Super profile)
 1. Velocette motorcycle
 I. Title II. Series
 629.2'275 TL448.V4

ISBN-0-85429-444-9

Cover design: Rowland Smith
Page Layout: Madaleine Bolton
Photographs: Andrew Morland and Author
Road tests: The Motor Cycle and Motor Cycling, courtesy of EMAP
Printed in England by:
J.H. Haynes & Co. Ltd

Titles in the *Super Profile* series

Ariel Square Four (F388)
BMW R69 & R69/S (F387)
Brough Superior SS100 (F365)
BSA A7 & A10 (F446)
BSA Bantam (F333)
Honda CB750 sohc (F351)
MV Agusta America (F334)
Norton Commando (F335)
Sunbeam S7 & S8 (F363)
Triumph Thunderbird (F353)
Triumph Trident (F352)

AC/Ford/Shelby Cobra (F381)
Austin-Healey 'Frogeye' Sprite (F343)
Corvette Stingray (F432)
Ferrari 250GTO (F308)
Fiat X1/9 (F341)
Ford Cortina 1600E (F310)
Ford GT40 (F332)
Jaguar E-Type (F370)
Jaguar D-Type & XKSS (F371)
Jaguar Mk 2 Saloons (F307)
Jaguar SS90 & SS100 (F372)
Lancia Stratos (F340)
Lotus Elan (F330)
Lotus Seven (F385)
MGB (F305)
MG Midget & Austin-Healey Sprite (except 'Frogeye') (F344)
Morris Minor Series MM (F412)
Morris Minor & 1000 (ohv) (F331)
Porsche 911 Carrera (F311)
Rolls-Royce Corniche (F411)
Triumph Stag (F342)

B29 Superfortress (F339)
Boeing 707 (F356)

Harrier (F357)
MIG 21 (F439)
Mosquito (F422)
Phantom II (F376)
P51 Mustang (F423)
Sea King (F377)
SEPECAT Jaguar (F438)
Super Etendard (F378)
Tiger Moth (F421)
Vulcan (F436)

Great Western Kings (F426)
Intercity 125 (F428)
V2 'Green Arrow' Class (F427)

Further titles in this series will be published at regular intervals. For information on new titles please contact your bookseller or write to the publisher.

Super Profile

FOREWORD

If I were asked to name my favourite motorcycle, I would find this a very difficult question to answer, because my allegiance extends to several different makes. But as far as the Velocette marque is concerned, the overhead camshaft models would take precedence, especially the KSS series which provided a unique blend of good road manners combined with the kind of performance you would expect from a race-bred thoroughbred. I have owned and worked on a goodly number of these machines in my time, and got to know their idiosyncrasies, not that there are many. I know better than to curse the Velocette clutch with its unorthodox method of adjustment which no one seems to understand, its starting problems, and the tendency for the crankcase to fill up with oil when the machine is left standing. All motorcycles have their shortcomings in one way or another, but the few possessed by the KSS Velocette are soon forgotten in the sheer joy of riding one of these models and in the pride of ownership. As I said to someone only the other day — British engineering at its best.

It is not an easy task to cover the history and development of a model that has enjoyed a production run of more than twenty years within the pages of a relatively small book. Yet on the other hand it is time the KSS models were singled out for special attention. Sadly, what should have been praise is now little more than an obituary; it seems difficult to believe that 35 years have passed since the last KSS model left the premises of Veloce Limited in York Road, Hall Green, Birmingham. The works themselves have gone too, with barely a trace left, another casualty in the demise of the British motorcycle industry. But if any machine made its mark, it was certainly the KSS Velocette, the brain child of Percy Goodman who brought the overhead camshaft engine within the reach of the average motorcyclist. Whilst motorcyclists many generations ahead may not need to be reminded of its existence, I hope my book will give an insight into what it is like to own and ride one of these machines, so that those who have only boxes of bits and pieces will be encouraged to reunite them and get yet another of these splendid models back on the road.

I would like to thank Ken Blake of Etna Motorcycles, Parkstone, for letting me have access to his early iron engine model for photographic purposes, also Pat Manley of Leigh, near Sherborne, for letting me do the same with his later, alloy engine model. Both are true enthusiasts who ride their machines on the road and take part in events whenever the opportunity presents itself. I would also like to thank George and Ethel Denley who, for so many years associated with Veloce Ltd, presented me with much historical information, including the early photographs I have used to accompany the text.

Jeff Clew

Super Profile

HISTORY

Although the first motorcycle to be designed and manufactured in its entirety by Veloce Limited was a four-stroke, it was mainly through the two-stroke designs that the company achieved its early reputation for quality and reliability. The original four-stroke design was advanced for its time, taking the form of a two-speed unit-construction engine mounted in a frame of conventional design. The engine was of the overhead inlet, side exhaust valve type, with belt drive to the rear wheel. A rocking pedal operated the two-speed gear and a later addition was a kickstarter. Percy Goodman, one of the two sons of the Goodman family, was responsible for the design, which was granted British Patent 24,499 on 21st October 1910. Sadly, sales were minimal — the design was far too advanced to be accepted by the conservatively-minded motorcyclists of that era. In consequence the company had to resort to manufacturing a close copy of the single-cylinder Triumph, in order to retain their foothold in the market.

Production of the four-strokes ceased when the manufacture of motorcycles for civilian use was prohibited during the Great War. When production resumed after the war, the company pursued a policy of two-strokes only until 1925.

The decision to manufacture another four-stroke machine was made as far back as 1923, when the Veloce board acknowledged the need to produce a higher powered model, in view of the heightening of interest in overhead valve engines which were capable of providing much better performance that their two-stroke counterparts. A better understanding of metallurgy had led to greater reliability so that the risk of a valve head breaking off its stem and dropping into the engine with consequent damage was greatly reduced. Already, the company had taken their 250cc two-stroke engines almost to the limit, it being acknowledged at that time that a two-stroke engine of greater than 250cc capacity was less efficient. Their experiments with a poppet-type valve in the crankcase to control the inlet charge more positively and hence produce more power had not proved a success. Engine seizures were frequent and there was the secondary problem of getting the valve action to follow the profile of the actuating cam, which ran at engine speed. The idea of using a disc valve as an alternative had been discarded. Another company employing this method of controlled induction had threatened Messrs Veloce Limited with legal action when one of their tentative ventures in this area had suggested that an infringement of patents could occur.

An incentive to give further consideration to a four-stroke design came about because the company needed a high class production model for the upper end of their range, which would uphold their reputation for quality and reliability, and perhaps enhance it by providing improved performance. There was also a need for better exhaust silencing (although the Velocette two-strokes were very good in this respect), without too much loss of power, and a general need for maximum enclosure of the working parts and their adequate lubrication. Most overhead valve engines at this time had exposed push-rods and valve gear, with only primitive and somewhat messy lubrication of the rocker arms by grease gun.

Once again it was Percy Goodman who came up with the answer, in the form of an overhead camshaft engine. Although he cannot be given credit for drawing up the first motorcycle engine with this type of layout, he did produce a really practical design that would form the basis of all future production models. JAP had an overhead camshaft engine as far back as 1914, and a double overhead camshaft design in 1922, which broke a remarkable number of records at Brooklands and other racing venues. But the JAP design never went into production, as did the Percy Goodman engine which, after some initial modifications, was granted British Patent 252,822 on 13th March 1925.

The Model K — prototype

The prototype design had a bore and stroke of 74 x 81mm, which gave a cubic capacity of 348cc. The overhead camshaft was driven by bevels connected by a vertical shaft that ran up the right-hand side of the cylinder barrel. Following conventional Veloce practice, the crankcase was kept very narrow by having the primary chain line inside that of the final drive chain, although this brought problems in its wake when it became apparent that a multi-plate clutch would be required. The prototype engine drove through a cork-lined, single-plate clutch attached to a modified version of the three-speed gearbox used for the 'H' series two-strokes, the clutch having face cam operation. A new frame had to be designed to accommodate the new engine, distinctive on account of its double front down tubes and the channel bracket behind the engine from which the gearbox was

5

Super Profile

suspended by two strong studs. The front forks were of the Druid type, with double springs, and the wheels of the beaded edge variety, with 650 x 65mm tyres.

The prototype was completed during 1924 and underwent a series of tests, which necessitated a number of modifications being made before it could be regarded as meeting the board's high expectations. Initially, the engine had a spindly look about it, with its scantily-finned cylinder head, parallel-sided magneto chaincase cover with no maker's identification, and the long, parallel-sided tube that enclosed the vertical coupling. Perhaps the most distinctive feature of all was the oil pump mounted on the cambox and driven off the left-hand extremity of the camshaft. The engine had been designed to run on the total loss lubrication principle, hence the pump was little more than a smaller version of the reciprocating pump used on the two-strokes, oil being fed from a separate compartment within the petrol tank.

The rate of flow was controlled by varying the stroke of the pump, oil being distributed to the rocker skids and cams, from whence it found its way to the bottom of the engine by passing down the vertical coupling tube. In practice, this lubrication system proved unacceptable because the oil failed to drain down the tube that contained the revolving shaft, preferring to build up around the top end of the shaft and the upper bevels. The bottom of the engine ran dry in consequence, with the inevitable problems of advanced wear and subsequent seizure.

Fortunately, the problem was solved relatively easily by reverting to dry sump lubrication, and placing a double gear pump in the right-hand crankcase half, driven from the mainshaft. At the same time the opportunity was taken to change from splines to Oldham couplings, the arrangement of coupling the vertical shaft to the upper and lower bevels. The use of a 'hunting tooth' layout ensured the heaviest loading did not occur consecutively on the same set of mating bevel teeth, but at the expense of making the valve timing much more difficult to achieve unless whoever disturbed it was aware of the need to follow an established routine. The cylinder head was provided with more generous fins, and the magneto chaincase cover and the vertical coupling tube took on a more pleasing appearance, the former bearing the legend 'Velocette' and 'Made in England'. The modified engine was installed in the frame used previously, and with the same cycle parts. It was catalogued as the Model K, and became available for the 1925 season.

The Model K – production

Contemporary reports were quite favourable, despite the fact that initially, the new model was marketed under the trade name Veloce. This had been the name used for the early four-strokes, the name Velocette having been adopted solely for the two-strokes. But by the time the Model K came onto the market, the Veloce name had been forgotten. Within a very short period of time it proved necessary to use the word Velocette, and from this point onwards sales increased significantly.

Teething troubles were experienced, as can be expected with any new design when it goes into general service. The screwed ring that retained the mainshaft shock absorber spring tended to unscrew itself, so that it would catch on the inside of the dome of the cast aluminium primary chain cover, wear its way through, then disappear over the hedge, effectively stopping all forward motion. A change from a right to a left-hand thread soon provided a permanent cure to this malady.

Valve spring breakages occurred too, such that it became necessary for the manufacturer to provide a small tool that could be attached to the lower tank rail so that the valve spring collars could be removed and the valve springs changed without the need to disturb either the cambox or the cylinder head. This was only a temporary expedient until such time as an alternative manufacturer was found who could supply more trustworthy springs. Petrol tank leakages were cured by finding an alternative manufacturer too, the 'tween the tubes' tanks of that period being of the soldered seam type.

Perhaps the most serious problem of all was that of oil leaks, which was partially cured by substituting a disc for the ball originally employed in the non-return valve fitted in the drain pipe from the cambox to the crankcase. But the main source of leakage – from the slots in the cambox through which the rocker arms extended to actuate the exposed valves and springs – could never be stopped completely. It was expecting too much of thin felt strips that acted as wipers to keep back hot oil at a pressure of about 8psi. As the late Arthur Lavington once said, "You can always tell the owner of an iron-engined ohc Velocette as he is the only one likely to wear waders in hot weather!" Leakage could also occur from the gland nuts of the vertical coupling, which were packed with several turns of asbestos string to help form a seal. Rubber sealing rings were tried unsuccessfully – although they provided an effective seal, they made the nuts almost impossible to unscrew after the machine had been in use for a while. Oil could sweat from the ends of the early rocker pins, until a change was made to those that screwed in. But even the screwed in variety gave cause for concern initially, as they would come unscrewed in use and disappear over the hedge like the early shock absorber screwed rings.

The knowledgeable soon learnt to drill them and either wire them together, or use a bicycle spoke bent up for the same purpose.

The question of oil leaks evidently caused the factory some concern, as the early instruction book gave advice on the very first page on how to cure them. It was not until Velocette's Service Manager, the late Bob Burgess, pointed out that this was hardly a good introduction of the owner to his ohc model that this advice was transferred to a later section.

As mentioned earlier, use of the original cork-lined single-plate clutch gave rise to problems, because the gearing of the primary drive created overloading due to its slow rotational speed. A change to a seven-plate clutch lined with composite friction material provided a complete answer, but only at the cost of overloading the gearbox pinions, which sometimes shed their teeth. A change to stub-tooth pinions soon stopped this too, the gearboxes so equipped having the prefix 'X' appended to their serial number. Evidently the early slip-prone clutch had acted as a safety valve.

It may seem that this frank exposition of the many early teething troubles suggests that the early Model K was anything but a success. One must take into account, however, that this model appeared on the scene during the so-called vintage period, when machines were not particularly oiltight and oil seals as we know them today had not been invented. Most new models had teething troubles of one kind or another at this time, and there were few 350s that had a maximum speed approaching 80mph or the high standard of roadholding and braking that had already become the hallmarks of Veloce Limited. The Model K soon earned for itself the reputation and status the board had anticipated when they drew up their original objectives.

During 1925, the decision was made to add a second model to the four-stroke range, a variant of the Model K that would have a guaranteed maximum speed of at least 80mph. It had not escaped the attention of the board that there was a demand for a machine with performance that would approach that of the models being raced in the TT, stripped of all but the bare legal necessities, for use on the public highways. Two Model Ks had been entered for the 1925 Junior TT and although neither finished, due to rocker arm breakages, much experience had been gained in preparing and testing these machines that could be applied to the new road-going version. And so the Model KSS came into being, the model that is the true ancestor of all the production ohc models that continued with this designation until the end of the 1948 season, apart from the obvious break in manufacture during World War 2.

The KSS is introduced

The first printed catalogue published by Veloce Limited in 1925 makes brief reference to the new overhead camshaft model in the Introduction, which reads as follows: 'For 1925 we have introduced a 2¾hp overhead camshaft four-stroke, capable of very high speeds. Some of its principal features are listed in the following pages.' Referring to these later pages, the constructional details are presented as follows, accompanied by an illustration of the original thin, spindly-looking engine:

'Since 1909 all Velocette engines have been fitted with a highly successful system of mechanical lubrication. The system of lubrication in the overhead camshaft engine is entirely mechanical, usually called dry sump lubrication. Oil is forced to the roller big end bearing, the camshaft, the bevel gears, and the overhead rockers. A detachable cylinder head is used, which can be removed without disturbing the engine in the frame. The camshaft casing is of special design, preventing leakage of oil. The aluminium piston is fitted with a scraper ring, and the gudgeon pin is floating. Large diameter valves are employed, made of cobalt chrome steel. The valve washers are held in position by split taper collars with annular grooves cut inside and engaging with similar grooves on the valve stem. This arrangement does not weaken the valve stem. The adjustable tappets give a rolling contact on the full width of the valve stem. A fine adjustment of valve timing is provided. The cams are of large dimensions. The drive to the overhead camshaft is flexible so that it can be easily and correctly refitted. A special piston can be supplied for racing purposes. The piston and con rod are as light as it is possible to make them.'

Strangely, the early 1925 catalogue has the Velocette logo above the constructional details section, whereas the later 1925-6 catalogue has the same copy, but features the modified and more shapely design of engine, with 'The Veloce' logo above it. This latter catalogue lists the Model K at £65, and what is described as the 'Super Sports Model KSS' at £75. A sports sidecar with frosted aluminium bodywork is listed at £18.

After the somewhat inauspicious début in the 1925 Junior TT, the overhead camshaft model made the headlines in a very big way when Alec Bennett rode one of these machines to victory in the 1926 Junior TT race, having established a lead of more than *ten minutes* over the second man home and attained a race average of 68.75mph. Many stories have been written about how Alec Bennett came to ride for Veloce Limited. The true version is that Alec saw such potential in the new overhead camshaft engine that he offered the factory his services as a rider on the

Super Profile

basis that if he won he would take all the money due to him, and if he failed in his objective he would take nothing. The two other factory riders, Gus Kuhn and Fred Povey, finished 5th and 9th respectively, which ensured that the factory won the Junior Team prize. So significant were these results that the factory soon needed to move to larger premises in York Road, Hall Green to cater for the orders that came flooding in for their overhead camshaft models.

The works-prepared TT machines had used the new seven-plate clutch lined with composite friction material and a revised method of clutch operation that employed the now familiar hinged thrust cup arrangement characteristic of Veloce design. It had not been easy to redesign the clutch to contain all the extra plates yet maintain the slim width that was essential if the inboard primary chain line was to be retained. These improvements were quickly passed on to the production models, thus illustrating the benefits achieved by taking part in competition events.

Within a relatively short period of time, a number of variants of the standard 'K' model appeared on the market, to provide alternative specifications at prices to suit the pocket of prospective purchasers. The cheapest was the Model KE, which had the same basic specification as the Model K, but was fitted with Brampton front forks and a steel chaincase in place of the cast aluminium oil bath. It retailed at £58. The Model K continued to retail at £65, but now had the benefit of Webb front forks, which it had inherited from the KSS model. For the more sporting type of rider there was the Model KS, the specification being similar to that of the Model K, but with narrower mudguards and tubular mudguard stays. It too retailed at £65.

To cater for the rider who required his machine mainly for touring purposes, there was the Model KT. It could be recognised by the footboards with which it was fitted, and often by the legshields, which were available as an optional extra on payment of an additional 30/-. The KT was another model that carried the £65 price tag.

The KSS model continued unchanged at £75, and was described as the machine 'which made rings around everything in the Junior TT'. As mentioned previously, 80mph was guaranteed, the power output being rated at 18-19bhp at 5,800rpm. A choice of two compression ratios was available at the time of ordering – 7:1 for 50% petrol/benzole or $8\frac{1}{2}$:1 for Discol PMS2 alcohol fuel. Supplied in full road-going trim, the KSS could be obtained, if required, with an open exhaust pipe of the correct length to give the best results for racing.

It was, of course, the KSS model that led to the eventual development of the KTT racing model, which is a story in itself. The KTT was the first really practical 'over-the-counter' racing model for sale to the general public, thereby establishing a completely new trend. There was also the short-lived and uncatalogued 'dirt track' model, which was little more than a KTT engine overbored to achieve a capacity of 415cc, fitted into a special frame and cycle parts for use on the cinders – this form of racing having made its debut in Britain during 1928. Perhaps best forgotten is the short diversion into a two exhaust port, coil ignition version of the 'K' engine, the result of an attempt to pander to public taste at the time when two bright, shiny exhaust pipes were all the rage. This was the infamous Model KTP, manufactured during 1930 and 1931 only, an aspect of the company's history most would like to forget. The basic design of the iron-engined overhead camshaft models continued virtually unchanged, with some rationalisation, until the end of the 1935 season. Some minor attention to the engine design had proved necessary during 1931, mainly due to the fact that these models were getting slower as a result of having to carry additional weight in the form of electric lighting equipment. But it was the advent of the 'M' series of push-rod models that highlighted the need for substantial redesign of the overhead camshaft models as there was little difference in performance between the KSS and MAC models, the latter representing a much cheaper purchase.

The Alloy Engine

The redesigned KSS model made its début during November 1935, to coincide with the Motor Cycle Show of that year. It differed in many respects from its predecessors in terms of both engine and cycle parts, even though the original bore and stroke dimensions of 74 x 81mm were retained. The engine now had the valve gear totally enclosed within a massive aluminium alloy cylinder head, and eccentric rocker pins facilitated valve clearance adjustment. The cylinder barrel was more generously finned and the magneto no longer base-mounted on a platform to its rear. Instead, the magneto was now attached by a flange mounting to the more substantial magneto chaincase cover. The inlet port was now downdraught, with a flange fitting carburetter to suit.

The frame was of entirely new construction, having a single down tube and a vertical saddle tube, forming a complete cradle underneath the engine. It was fitted with heavier weight Webb girder forks having tapering tubes as their main recognition feature. Engine and gearbox were united by substantial engine plates and arranged so that the engine and gearbox could be lifted out in unison. The gearbox was of improved design too, with a better means of mounting and improved method of adjustment. Otherwise, it was similar in some respects to the four-speed boxes fitted to the later iron-engined models that had an internal positive-stop mechanism. The KSS frame was, in fact, identical to that used for the 495cc MSS model, which had come on to the market earlier that year.

Like its iron-engined predecessor, the new KSS engine had its teething problems too, having a tendency to burn oil. Changes to a slipper piston and a slotted oil control ring brought about a significant improvement, as did valve guide seals. Perhaps of more serious consequence was an epidemic of valve spring breakages, pieces of which would pass into the oil pump and shear the drive. Close-coil valve springs obviated the problem, but as a further safeguard, a small conical filter was fitted to the end of the drain pipe from the cylinder head. From 1939 onwards, the addition of a suction filter provided an even more permanent safeguard. Even with all these problems rectified, the alloy engined KSS models were by no means super-fast. At one stage, models coming off the production line would barely reach 70mph, and in consequence Ted Mellors, the 'works' road racer, was involved with road testing. Contrary to popular belief, the standard KSS model has never been a particularly fast machine, 72-75mph being its maximum speed in most cases. But unlike its predecessors, it could be made oiltight with very little effort, and it was certainly very much quieter mechanically.

World War 2 interrupted production but in 1947 the KSS was back on the market, though without its alternative touring version, the KTS. A major problem arose at the end of that season when Webb announced they were to discontinue making their girder front fork. Fortunately, Dowty Equipment offered an alternative in the form of air-controlled telescopic forks with oil damping, obviating the use of internal springs. The KSS continued for one more year, so equipped, until production came to an end in 1948. The overhead camshaft model had become too expensive to make, as it was not suited to production line methods on account of the need for hand assembly when meshing the bevels of the camshaft drive, a time consuming task if it was to be carried out correctly. There were many who mourned the passing of the KSS (and with it the production KTT model), especially when the new addition to the Veloce range was a 150cc water-cooled horizontally opposed four stroke lightweight. Apart from the war years, the overhead camshaft model had been in production since 1925, long enough to endear itself to those who had ridden one of these machines, and to carve for itself a niche in the history of the British motorcycle. It is still remembered with affection today, and has become one of the most prized acquisitions in this, the collectors' era.

Super Profile

EVOLUTION

The first production 'K' models came on to the market during 1925, initially fitted with the original spindly-looking engine that had been modified to dry sump lubrication. It would seem probable that very few of these machines were made, as none appears to have survived. The revised engine design made its appearance shortly afterwards, and at least one of these models is in existence today, having been fully restored. The specification comprises the twin down tube frame with Druid front forks, the early wedge-type petrol tank, wheels shod with beaded edge tyres and the early gearbox with the face cam operated clutch. Appropriately, the petrol tank has 'The Veloce' transfers.

The KSS sports version of the Model K was first listed in the 1925-6 catalogue, which became available late in 1925, but it was not until the 1926 Motor Cycle Show that it really came into prominence as a result of the company's Junior TT win. Catalogued as the KSS model, it was referred to by the press as the 'TT' model, and it presented a particularly handsome appearance by making use of a saddle tank for the first time. Webb front forks had replaced the earlier Druid forks, and it and the standard Model K now made use of a new and more efficient silencer, the so-called 'water bottle' design. Wire-bead tyres had now superseded the beaded edge variety.

By 1927, several variants of the standard Model K became available, chiefly the slightly cheaper KE model fitted with Brampton forks, the KS model, in effect a cross between the K and KSS models, and the KT model, which was a touring version fitted with footboards and with the option of legshields. The range broadened still further in 1928, by which time the company had won their second Junior TT. All models now had saddle tanks and Webb front forks, and all were available with electric lighting as an optional extra, involving the fitting of either a Lucas Magdyno or a BTH Mag Generator Type PB. The newcomer to the range was the Model KES, which had the same specification as the cheaper KE model, apart from the use of narrow mudguards and tubular mudguard stays. Some models, such as the K, KE and KES now had slightly smaller diameter wheel rims, and were fitted with wider section tyres. Changes were made to the frame design in the form of larger diameter steering head races and by having a pronounced 'kink' in the lower tank tube to make cambox removal much easier. Prices were rising. The cheapest models, the KE and the KES, retailed at £61, whilst the top of the range KSS was now priced at £78.15s. The Model K was dropped from production at the end of the year.

Model designations changed for the 1929 season, following the introduction of the KTT racing model. The KSS model continued virtually unchanged, not yet having the option of the foot controlled gearchange fitted to the KTT models. Two cheaper models of almost identical specification replaced the earlier K variants, the KN and the KNS – the former having a luggage carrier and slightly different pattern mudguards. Electrics were still an option; the KN and KNS models retailed at £62.10s, against the £70 of the KSS model. By now, the ohc Velocette had become the fastest 350 in the world, due to a successful bid for world records in 1928 by H.J. Willis, F.G. Hicks and J.A. Baker. No less than 50 world records were taken on the occasion of this session at Montlhéry, including the hour at a record average speed of 100.39mph. Another Junior TT win in 1929, with 1st, 3rd, 5th, 6th, 7th, 10th and 11th placings, provided the final seal of success.

By 1930, the overhead camshaft range had been reduced to just two models, with a reduction in price, for the depression of the late twenties was having its effect. The KSS model was down to £62.10s, with the option of Miller S.U.S. electric lighting for an extra £5.5s. The other model was the infamous KTP, which had coil ignition with the dynamo behind the cylinder barrel and the contact breaker driven off the left-hand end of the camshaft. A special pear-shaped timing cover enclosed the drive gear needed to speed up the dynamo from the half engine speed previously needed for the magneto. A twin-port cylinder head was another feature, the exhaust pipes ending in neat, fishtail-ended silencers. Complete with electric lighting, the KTP retailed at £58, the cheapest ohc Velocette yet. The same two models continued unchanged for 1931, although this proved to be the last year of manufacture of the KTP. It had never been as popular as intended, having a lower performance than the single exhaust port models and a tendency for oil to spread over the contact breaker points.

A certain amount of redesign proved necessary during 1931, in order to improve performance. The addition of lighting equipment and its extra weight had made this move necessary, which outwardly was not very evident. The machines were still fitted with hand

10

gearchange as standard, but there was the option of the positive-stop foot gearchange at extra cost, TT racing footrests, and a high level exhaust pipe.

The KSS model fell in price again during 1932, coming complete with lighting for only £56. A face lift had been given by a deeper and more shapely 4 gallon petrol tank and the adoption of the fishtail silencer à la KTP. The side-mounted oil tank now became a standard fitting, instead of being used only when lighting was fitted to make room for the battery. A second ohc model became available this year, the KTS. Marketed at the same price as the KSS, it differed only in respect of tyre sizes and mudguards. It was intended primarily for touring, or for the attachment of a sidecar.

1933 brought about another significant change in the form of a four-speed gearbox fitted to both the KSS and KTS models, with a new design of kickstarter mechanism and a kickstarter with a folding crank. It was of the hand change type, but could be adapted to foot change by fitting the optional bolt-on unit with its own positive-stop mechanism. Both models now retailed at £57.

A further change in gearbox design occurred during 1934, when it was again redesigned so that the positive-stop gearchange mechanism could be contained internally, thus dispensing with the bolt-on circular box used previously. The gearchange lever now pivoted from a bushed lug at the top of the gearbox end-cover casting, with an external linkage to the external gear operating arm, as before. Footchange was now a standard fitment, and not an option. With the advent of the push rod MAC model that retailed at only £49.10s, against £59.10s of the KSS and KTS models, doubts were being expressed about the performance of the ohc models which was being matched by their cheaper counterpart. A BTH magneto now became part of the standard specification, and the KSS model was officially credited with a maximum speed of 75mph.

The iron-engined KSS and KTS models came to the end of their production run at the end of 1935, without any further changes in specification being made. The price of both had risen slightly to £61, but there was still a price differential of £10 between them and the lower-priced push-rod MAC model.

For a very brief period there was, technically speaking, a break in production before the new alloy-engined KSS and KTS models made their début just before the 1935 Motor Cycle Show, at which the 1936 models were launched. But this was scarcely noticeable in the trade and to all intents and purposes can be disregarded as the period was so short. Models already in stock were sufficient to bridge the gap.

Not unexpectedly, the new alloy-engined KSS and KTS models caused quite a sensation when they were launched. Differing in so many respects from their iron-engined predecessors, they presented a very handsome appearance, seeming to have a closer affinity with the company's racing models. The engine had the same bore and stroke dimensions, and used a few parts of the original design, but there were many other differences, including a really beautifully-cast alloy cylinder head that totally enclosed the valve gear. The frame was entirely new and identical to that of the MSS model, having a single down tube, a vertical saddle tube and a full cradle under the engine. It was fitted with heavyweight Webb girder forks having tapering tubes and the gearbox was no longer suspended by two studs but instead attached to the rear engine plates so that it could be lifted out in unison with the engine, and the complete primary drive. The dynamo, still belt driven from an engine pulley, was mounted higher up in front of the engine and still of Miller origin. An $8\frac{1}{4}$ inch headlamp was fitted. Other changes in specification included a downdraught carburetter fitted with an easy starting device and a longer and more handsome fishtail silencer that became the 'classic' Velocette design. Despite all these innovations, the two new models retailed at only £62.10s., the KSS model retaining the larger diameter wheels and narrower mudguards.

Few changes in specification were made to either model until production came to a temporary halt early in 1940, due to World War 2. Teething troubles brought about some changes in the way in which oil was metered to the top bevel housing, a short, external pipe leading to a 'quill' in the cambox cover being used for a brief period. There were also changes to close-coil valve springs and the use of leather seals at the top of the valve guides, the last to help reduce oil consumption. In 1938, the Miller dynamo was changed to the two-brush type, with voltage control. The 1939 models and all those made afterwards can be recognised by the suction filter incorporated in the bottom portion of the right-hand crankcase half, which has given special builders problems due to the extra frame clearance needed when another type of frame is used. The 1939 and later models also had a different type of side damper adjuster on the front forks. It took the form of a round knob, rather like that used on old domestic radiators.

The KSS model only was made after the war, production recommencing late in 1946. The cylinder head had the advantage of a slightly larger inlet valve, a change that had been made to the very last pre-war models commencing with engine number 8972. All post-war engine numbers were from 10,000 onwards. Another small change affected the gearbox, the internal camplate having been changed so that the gearchange was now 'down for up' and 'up for down', to correspond with the action of most other post-war machines. Most noticeable was the new price – £139, and exclusive of the newly-introduced purchase tax at that!

The last change of all took place during 1948, and was brought about because the manufacture of Webb girder front forks had been discontinued. Instead, a Dowty 'Oleomatic' telescopic front fork was fitted, which relied upon compressed air as its main suspension medium and contained no internal springs. The use of this fork, which was fitted to all the other Velocette models in production at that time, necessitated a different shape of petrol tank, tapered more at the front to give sufficient clearance when the forks were on full lock. A 19 inch diameter front wheel with an alloy brake plate was fitted, and it was necessary to transfer the speedometer drive to a gearbox driven by the rear wheel and through which the rear wheel spindle passed. This proved to be the only year in which the KSS model was fitted with telescopic front forks. Production ceased at the end of 1948, as part of a move to make way for the new 150cc water-cooled twin – the LE Velocette. Sales had become minimal; the KSS had proved to be too costly and too time consuming to make 23 years after its birth.

In conclusion, it should be said that the foregoing is only a brief description of the design changes made over the years and does not cover every single point in detail. Furthermore, it should be remembered that the years quoted are not necessarily calendar years but manufacturing years, most manufacturers starting to make the forthcoming season's models as early as 1st September the preceding year. Even then, modifications tended to be made gradually, in order to use up stocks of existing components, and to save disclosing some of their newer innovations to their rivals until the official launch which, as often as not, was planned for the eve of the annual Motor Cycle Show.

It is also pertinent to mention that the KTS models were always fitted with an engine that had a KSS engine number prefix. A KTS prefix was never used in this respect, a fact that has caused KTS owners some concern when trying to establish whether their machine is fully authentic.

Super Profile

SPECIFICATION

	1929/30	1938/39
Bore and stroke	74 x 81mm	74 x 81mm
Cubic capacity	348cc	348cc
Compression ratio	7:1 or 8.5:1[1]	7.5:1 or 8.4:1[2]
bhp	18-19 @ 5,800rpm	N/A
Gear ratios[3]		
4th	—	6.02
3rd	5.55	7.26
2nd	7.95	9.55
1st	13.90	13.80
Sprocket sizes		
Engine	20	21
Clutch	44	44
Final drive*	22	16
Rear wheel	56	46
Tyre sizes		
Front (KSS)	21 x 2.75	21 x 3.00
Rear (KSS)	21 x 2.75	20 x 3.25
Front (KTS)	19 x 3.25 (1932-5)	19 x 3.25
Rear (KTS)	19 x 3.25 (1932-5)	19 x 3.50
Suspension		
Front	Webb girder forks	Webb girder forks
Rear	Rigid	Rigid
Brake drum diameter		
Front	7in	7in
Rear	7in	7in
Chain size		
Primary	0.5in x 0.305in	0.5in x 0.305in
Secondary	0.5in x 0.305in	0.625in x 0.380in

Super Profile

Fuel tank capacity	2¼ gall (Imp)	3½ gall (Imp)
Ignition system	ML magneto	BTH magneto
Points gap	0.012in	0.012in
Timing (BTDC)	42°	40°
Electrical system		
Dynamo	Miller DM3G[4]	Miller DVR[5]
Output	45 watts	45 watts
Valve timing		
Inlet opens (BTDC)	40°[6]	35°[7]
Inlet closes (ABDC)	56°	65°
Exhaust opens (BBDC)	68°	70°
Exhaust closes (ATDC)	47°	30°
Ground clearance	4½in	4½in
Dimensions		
Seat height	28in	28in
Overall width	29in	27½in
Wheelbase	55¾in	55in
Weight	265lb	340lb

Notes

*The final drive sprocket is the only sprocket that can be varied in size to change the overall gear ratios (as for use with a sidecar).

1. Compression ratio can be varied by changing piston to suit fuel being used. Lowest ratio 6:1 for standard fuel, 7:1 for petrol/benzole.
2. Compression ratio on later models can be varied by adding or removing compression plates under cylinder barrel.
3. These ratios apply when standard size final drive sprocket is fitted.
4. Three-brush dynamo.
5. Two-brush dynamo with separate voltage control unit.
6. With K17/2 cam fitted. Special valve clearances needed when checking timing.
7. With K17/7 cam fitted. Special valve clearances needed when checking timing.

Guide to Engine Numbers

Early engines have prefix 'K' only. 'C' in engine number prefix denotes later type of cams, 'R' later type of rocker arms, and 'N' new type of big-end.

Racing models identified by KTT engine number prefix and externally-ribbed crankcase. Rare dirt track model had KDT engine number prefix. All KTP engines have KA engine number prefix.

The KTS engine number prefix was *NOT* used, hence all KTS models have an engine with a KSS engine number prefix. All post-war engine numbers commence from 10 000.

The use of the designations Mark I for the iron engine models, and Mark II for the alloy engine models was never in official use at the factory. It has come into use as a convenient means of distinguishing between the pre- and post-1936 models, the former being the direct descendants of the original 1925 Model K.

14

ROAD TESTS

The front panel of a 1928 catalogue showing two ohc models

ROAD TESTS OF 1932 MODELS

The 348 c.c. o.h.c.
VELOCETTE

The New K.T.S. Model Proves a Delightful Machine for Fast Road Work

WHEN a road test of a K.T.S. overhead camshaft Velocette was embarked upon it was not difficult to guess that it would be enjoyable, but, for once in this imperfect world, realization exceeded anticipation. It was a most delightful machine in every respect.

First and foremost it is the engine which is remarkable. There is something about the extraordinary smoothness of this marvellous o.h.c. unit that puts it in a class by itself. To talk of the "roughness" of a single cylinder is impossible after riding such a machine.

We were able to cover a useful mileage on this machine, close on 1,000 miles in all, mostly with the plate under the cylinder, but for a while with it removed. In its lower compression form the machine was more pleasant for average conditions, and the performance was hardly altered with the plate inserted. Unless the very last ounce of speed is required it would be as well to retain it in position.

A 75 m.p.h. Maximum.

In this form it was found that the maximum speed was within a fraction of 75 m.p.h. This was accomplished on several occasions, but it necessitated the rider, clad in a large coat, lying down to it to reduce the wind resistance. An honest 70 m.p.h. could be obtained at any time and in a very short distance, and at this speed there is not the slightest vibration, nor any sign that the engine is not thoroughly enjoying itself.

The acceleration was excellent, but with a wide-ratio box nothing terrific could be done on bottom gear. In second, however, 55 m.p.h. was often exceeded up considerable main-road hills. The performance, then, would be out of the way even for an expensive 350, and the Velocette is not an expensive machine. And it is obtained without super tuning and without the risk that after a few hundreds of miles have been rolled off on the Smith-Jaeger speedometer (mounted where it can be seen on the front forks), the m.p.h. will drop off; on the contrary, the K.T.S. is built to remain capable of giving of its best over very long periods without attention. Certainly at the end of the 1,000 miles that it was ridden in our hands it was faster than it had been at the beginning.

Their racing experience year by year has allowed the Velocette designers to improve the performance of standard engines, and for 1932 the internal modifications have been numerous. That they have proved satisfactory will be realized by everybody who rides one of these new models.

Delightful Steering.

As noteworthy as the engine is the steering. If there is a better steering machine on the market it must be a marvel. The rider feels that it is impossible to do anything wrong on the road. Hands off at 70 m.p.h. is the easiest possible feat; wrong cambers, manholes, drains make no difference; it just steers itself, and the slightest wobble, even with the steering damper completely slack, is quite unthinkable. The riding position of the 1932 models is a trifle lower than that of previous Velocettes, nevertheless, it is still rather higher than the average run of motorcycles, and therein, no doubt, is one of the secrets of the phenomenal steering. Whatever it is—and the Webb forks are certainly due for their share of the praise—the result is something to wonder at and to delight in.

On one occasion a journey from Gloucester to the suburbs of Birmingham was made in an hour and ten minutes to the amazement of the rider, who had in no way been "trying." This average (you can work it out for yourself!) was all the more remarkable because the roads were just about as greasy as they could be, and there was a good deal of fog about at the time. Yet it did not seem as if any "fast motoring" was being done, and never once was there a trace of even a modest skid. With such an engine and such steering, even the most restrained motorcyclist cannot help putting up fast averages.

It is sometimes said that if a machine is a really first-class main road steerer it is "no good on rough stuff." The Velocette refutes even this light impeachment. Used for reporting both the Reliance and British Experts' events it had its fair share of trials' going, and it acquitted itself perfectly satisfactorily. One example from each event may be mentioned. In the former it climbed the difficult grass-grown Vron, near Llangollen, which gave trouble to many competitors, flat-out in bottom gear at a very decent speed, without even a trace of tail-wag, while in the latter, again despite the absence of competition tyres, the top part of Lypiatt was tackled and a non-stop ascent managed.

I.O.M.-bred Brakes.

The third essential of any machine with speed capabilities is reliable brakes, and here, too, nothing but praise can be given. The pedal controlling the rear brake is perfectly positioned and there is just that high standard of efficiency that one would expect an Island-bred machine to possess. After one application the rider is in possession of a feeling of complete confidence.

At first the model under review proved rather a difficult starter during a cold spell. A vast improvement was obtained by substituting a different brand of oil. One of the secrets of this power unit is the large quantity of lubricant in circulation, and unless a fairly "thin" grade is used there is some difficulty in turning the engine over when it is cold. When warm, it is a certain "first-kicker."

"Clean" handlebars are fitted, and the magneto is controlled by the left twist-grip. When, at our suggestion, this had been made to advance the magneto timing when opened inwards (so that the brain did not have to cope with two differently operating movements), the rider felt happier, but the principle of a twist-grip for this control seems to have little to recommend it.

It is not easy to use the clutch and retard the magneto at the same time, and, in practice, it is often desirable to do so. Further, with a twist grip one cannot tell accurately the degree of advance or retard by the "feel" of the control or by looking at it.

Powerful Lighting.

The Miller S.U.S. lighting gave every satisfaction and a splendid beam. As previously mentioned in road tests, the switch operating the dual filament bulb has a disconcerting trick of sticking in a "neutral" position. Oddly enough, two rear bulbs broke, but this must be considered pure bad luck. The "Clear-Hooter" electric horn gave a really pleasing and penetrating note, and was one of the best English electric horns which we have tried.

Mechanical noises and—thanks to the chaincase—transmission sounds were negligible, and the exhaust note was subdued enough to disarm the most critical. A slight rattle somewhere at the rear occurred at about 55 m.p.h., but this could not be traced.

For 1932 two standard examples of the camshaft Velocette are offered, the model tested and the K.S.S., which differs only as regards the tyre and mudguard sizes. The larger guards, fitted to the K.T.S., proved very effective in extremely muddy conditions.

The discriminating rider, with £56 to spend, would be well advised to take a run on a K.T.S.

(Above) The dynamo of the Miller S.U.S. lighting system is mounted in front of the crankcase and driven by a totally enclosed leather belt. The primary chain is also fully enclosed. (Right) Even for a very tall rider the Velocette affords a comfortable riding position.

1940 Models on the Road

The 350 c.c.

The "handling, steering and braking" of the Velocette "were all superb."

The Velocette KSS machine looks the real thoroughbred that it is. The overhead camshaft engine is renowned for its exceptionally smooth running.

IN these days of petrol shortage and treacherous roads it was a real pleasure to have a glorious day of freedom on a KSS Velocette. Whilst surfaces were icy there was ample opportunity to appreciate the stability and good handling of this famous 350, but discretion had to be exercised with the throttle and all corners negotiated with the machine vertical. Imagine, therefore, our tester's joy when a thaw set in and it was possible to sally forth on normal roads, for the purpose of logging a series of consumption figures and covering sufficient miles to obtain a true impression of the Velocette's handling and performance.

Good things were expected, but when all expectations are surpassed enthusiasm is apt to gain the upper hand, so if this road test appears to be nothing but a list of praises will the reader please make a mental note that they are true and considered impressions well earned by a first-class machine.

Whilst the test followed our normal procedure, special attention was given to the matter of fuel consumption and the results obtained were remarkably good. Even the dragging hand of Pool petrol does not dull the performance or ruin the economy, provided, of course, reasonable speeds are used when attempting to travel the greatest distance on the smallest possible amount of fuel. For instance, travelling at a steady 30 m.p.h. the result was 105 m.p.g. Using a top speed of 40 m.p.h., and averaging 35 m.p.h. over 21 miles of give-and-take roads, the figure was 91 m.p.g., whilst a cruising speed of 50-55 m.p.h. when possible, produced the handsome average speed of 45.8 m.p.h. and a consumption of 76 m.p.g.

The KSS was then ridden as fast as possible, with the rider normally seated. A quart of fuel was placed in the test tank, the changes up were made at 45 and 60 m.p.h. from second and third respectively, and a maximum in top of 68 m.p.h. was reached several times. In 12 minutes 26 seconds the fuel ran out after 12.2 miles had been covered. Very extravagant, but what a glorious spell!

From these results emerges one interesting point. Averaging 30 m.p.h. the consumption was just over 100 m.p.g. Double the average speed by riding flat out and the consumption figure is almost exactly halved. Such is the cost of speed.

All these results were obtained with the taper needle in the carburetter lowered one notch from standard, and after the compression ratio had been lowered by placing one extra compression plate under the cylinder base. One was fitted in the first case, but the high compression ratio argued in a loud voice with Mr. Pool; the extra plate made the engine run sweeter and pinking only occurred when running slowly with the ignition on full advance.

Oil consumption was practically negligible, half a pint being needed after a distance of 210 miles. Certainly there was no external wastage of this commodity as all the works remained spotlessly clean and the gearbox retained its pristine beauty in the same manner.

Having completed the consumption tests the KSS was taken to the measured quarter mile and batted up and down the straight four times, to return a mean timed speed of 76.27 m.p.h., with an average of two runs in one direction of 78.2 m.p.h. In third and second gears the engine gave off its power in the same smooth and efficient manner, the respective speeds being 68 m.p.h. and 54 m.p.h., both of which represent over 6,000 r.p.m. A standing quarter mile in 19.3 secs., or at 46.63 m.p.h., is also most excellent for a 350, particularly on a greasy road, which caused quite a bit of wheel spin on the starting line. At no time were

February 8, 1940.   Motor Cycling

KSS VELOCETTE

A Special Consumption Test Produces Excellent "All-in" M.P.G. Figures

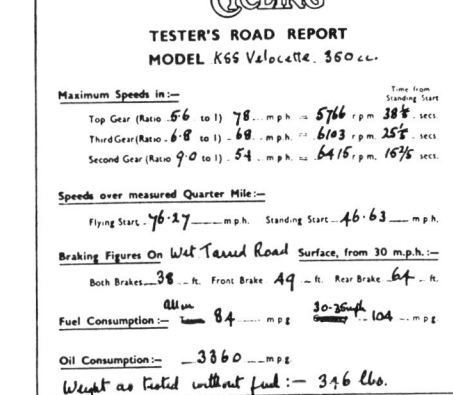

The main performance figures of the KSS are given in this chart. As will be seen, it covered the flying quarter at over 76 m.p.h.

there any traces of vibration, whilst the pulling powers were good at slow speeds and the transmission was free from snatch down to 13 m.p.h. in top, 10 m.p.h. in third and below the speedometer reading in second.

Starting caused a little trouble when the thermometer was hovering about 20 degrees F. below freezing point; however, a few ways and means produced the desired effect, at the third or fourth kick, which briefly were as follow. Flood the carburetter, close the air, turn up the quickly adjustable throttle stop, and then kick the engine over three or four times with the throttle *wide open*. Close it back against the stop, get the engine on to compression, and give one smart prod. Hey Presto, and the baby is alive! When the engine was hot a single kick started it at a delightfully quiet tick over, more representative of a woolly side valve than a high-performance o.h.c. motor.

Handling, steering and braking were all superb. The Velocette was a real joy to ride under all normal conditions, and even on snow and ice it was markedly easier to manage

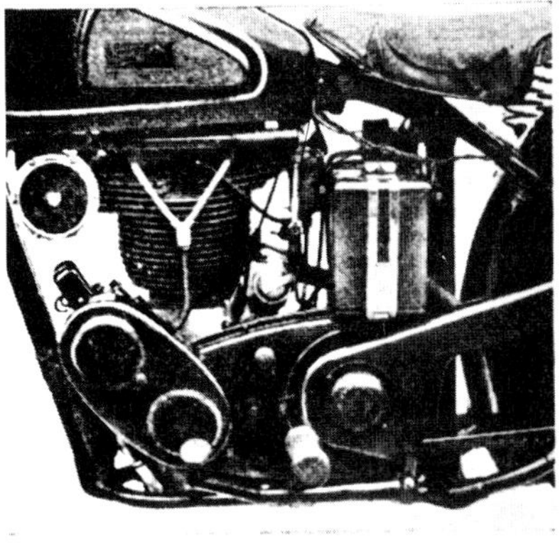

This close-up view of the near side of the KSS shows the cases enclosing the dynamo and primary drives, the accessibility of the battery, the long brake lever, the oil feeds to the rear chain and to the overhead camshaft box.

BRIEF SPECIFICATION OF THE KSS VELOCETTE
Engine: Velocette single-port overhead camshaft; 74 mm. bore, 81 mm. stroke = 348 c.c. Aluminium alloy head cast integral with the rocker box. Rocker gear totally enclosed and positively lubricated. Dry sump lubrication. Amal carburetter with push-pull control. Magneto ignition.
Transmission: ½-in. by .305-in. primary running in oil-bath. ⅝-in. by .380-in. rear lubricated by crankcase breather. Engine shaft shock absorber. Gear ratios with 17-tooth sprocket: 5.6, 6.8, 9.0 and 13.0 to 1. Foot change, folding kick-starter.
Frame: Cradle type. Brazed joints. Sidecar lugs incorporated. Tubular front forks with bronze bushes and ground spindles. Shock absorber incorporated.
Wheels: 3.00 by 21 front, 3.25 by 20 rear. Rear wheel quickly detachable, front and rear brakes 7 ins. by 1 in.
Tanks: Petrol, 3½ gallons. Oil, ½ gallon carried under saddle.
Dimensions: Wheelbase, 55 ins. Saddle height, 28 ins. Ground clearance, 4½ ins. Overall width, 27½ ins. Overall length, 84 ins. Weight, 346 lb.
Equipment: 120 m.p.h. speedometer. Separate dynamo, belt driven. 8½-in. head lamp, horn, tool kit, spring-top saddle, pillion and footrests, prop stand.
Price: £83. No extras.
Makers: Veloce, Ltd., York Road, Hall Green, Birmingham.

than most machines. It was a pleasure to use in towns, for the steering was light yet quite definite about keeping straight when the surface was composed of greasy cobbles.

On the open road it was a thrill to be astride the KSS, particularly when there was any rapid cornering to be done. If ever a machine felt as though it was on rails, this was the one. It did not seem to matter whether the surface was wavy, smooth or bumpy, the behaviour was beyond any criticism when it is remembered that a rigid frame is used. A steering damper was fitted, but no benefit could be derived from its use under any of the circumstances which were encountered.

A good riding position made long distances comfortable, and an exceptionally smooth and powerful pair of brakes made for a nicety of control which is so often part and parcel of race-bred machines. Excellent results were obtained with 20 lb. per sq. in. in the front and 18 lb. per sq. in. in the rear tyre.

Yet another point which made the KSS a pleasure to ride was the unusual degree of silence. Mechanically it proved to be one of the quietest road-test machines that have been through our hands, whilst the exhaust was at all times unobtrusive to the rider and would attract no untimely comment from an outsider, unless he was prejudiced against a motorcycle as such.

Maintenance

From the maintenance point of view there should be little trouble. Both chains were easily tensioned with the tools provided in the kit and the dynamo belt could be checked and tightened in a matter of three minutes. It was necessary to raise the tank to get at the valve adjusters; this, however, was simple and in any case a job which is unlikely in between decokes. The battery was handy and the rear wheel could be removed and replaced in under five minutes, leaving the brake drum and sprocket in situ the while.

Following normal Velocette practice, the equipment was complete, including a pillion seat and rests, whilst the workmanship and finish were excellent. The cost is £83, a high figure, maybe, but after riding such a machine and appreciating its good points to the full, anyone with the money to spare would have a gem with which he would be loath to part.

Super Profile

OWNER'S VIEW

Introduction

Having rebuilt and restored a considerable number of both the iron engine and alloy engine KSS models, I feel well qualified to present my own views as a preface to this section of the book. Of the two, I have come to prefer the early models, despite their tendency to leak oil even after very careful assembly. Their lean appearance makes them look much more attractive and their lighter weight gives a more favourable power-to-weight ratio, which results in a better overall performance. Any carefully assembled KSS of the 1927-30 period should be capable of about 80mph on standard pump fuel, when in standard trim and fully-equipped for normal road use. Furthermore, the standard of roadholding and braking that can be expected far exceeds that which was commonplace amongst most other machines during this period of manufacture. Although one hears of quite exceptional performance from the alloy engine models made from 1936 onwards, it is a plain statement of fact that 75mph represents the usual maximum speed that can be expected from a standard model of this type.

It is, of course, possible to improve the performance of either category of model without too much difficulty. Apart from the requirement for careful assembly in good working conditions, the high degree of interchangeability of Velocette parts makes possible the use of later parts in some of the earlier models, and in the case of the later models, parts from the KTT racing machines. Perhaps I can illustrate this by quoting two examples.

In the mid-1950s, when I was involved with vintage racing, I constructed a hybrid that comprised a 1930 KTP frame and cycle parts, into which was fitted a KTP engine that I had converted to KSS specification. The main reason for using the KTP frame and cycle parts, apart from their being readily to hand, was that it was much easier to obtain 19 inch racing tyres than the standard 21 inch items and that the frame and forks were, if anything, slightly lighter in weight. Carefully assembled and run on 73 octane pump fuel, using the original cams, a speedometer reading of fractionally over 80mph could be obtained along the top straight at Brands Hatch. The gearing was standard too, the only concession to racing being the use of an open exhaust pipe of the correct length. The handling characteristics were unbelievably good for a machine of this age, as were the brakes, which became a vital necessity when the machine shed its secondary chain as I started to ease up for the notorious Paddock Bend!

At the other end of the scale, it was during the early 1960s that I purchased a quite standard 1938 model at the time when I had joined the BEMSEE team of travelling marshals. I decided to modify it progressively between race meetings so that eventually I would have the equivalent of what I considered would have been the 1963 version, had production of this model continued after 1948. The final specification included the original front half of the frame with a McKenzie swinging arm conversion added at the rear, using Girling dampers, Velocette telescopic front forks, Venom wheels with full-width hubs, and a fully-valanced rear mudguard fitted with a dual seat. The engine had been fitted with a post-war cylinder head used in a Clubman's TT by the late Arthur Lavington, to take advantage of the larger inlet valve, an 'Alfin' alloy cylinder barrel, a Lucas 60 watt dynamo with matching voltage control unit, driven by a Venom vee belt and pulleys, and an Amal Monobloc carburetter. This last modification necessitated dispensing with the standard oil tank and replacing it with the MOV type, to give the new carburetter room to breathe. It also presented the opportunity to fit the Venom one-way valve to shut off the oil flow when the engine stopped. Needless to say, these modifications caused the machine to get a little overweight, so the use of a K17/8 cam from a Mark VIII KTT helped restore the balance. With full lighting equipment and a Venom-type silencer (the machine was often ridden to race meetings in the early hours of the morning), the speedometer would read just over 90mph along Hangar Straight at Silverstone, whilst I was sitting bolt upright. Roadholding and braking were good, especially the latter with the wide linings of the Venom front brake. But although quite acceptable and always giving a feeling of confidence, the roadholding was never quite up to the standard of the earlier models.

My infatuation with the ohc models began way back in 1952, when a friend offered to exchange two 1928 models for the 1927 Model 18 Norton I had at that time. One machine was more or less complete, the other completely dismantled. The former was alleged to have been owned by Stanley Woods at one time, which I now believe was untrue! But it had a KCR engine number prefix, which I quite incorrectly assumed meant it was a racing model. To cut a long story short, I fell for the offer and thus commenced a long involvement with the ohc Velocettes that continues today.

Like most newly-acquired machines, the assembled KSS needed a complete rebuild to make it run in a satisfactory and reliable manner. Perhaps it was as well, for I soon learnt how to retime the valves without falling foul of the hunting tooth arrangement, and how to adjust the Velocette clutch that has been the downfall of many a backyard enthusiast. Parts were no problem, with a spare machine to hand. But had I needed anything, the early parts were still reasonably easy to obtain at that time, even direct from the factory. Most faults could be attributed to earlier 'hammer and chisel' owners and their total ignorance of the finer workings of the Velocette engine. I was most impressed by the thoughtfulness that had gone into the basic design and the precision with which the parts had been made.

The standard of performance and the general handling qualities proved quite an eye-opener, once the machine was on the road. One must recall that I was comparing this with a previously-owned 500cc Norton. The machine was raced on several occasions, mainly in sprint meetings at venues such as Trent Park, Cockfosters, and Sampford and Abridge, both in Essex. Invariably, it was hacked to and from meetings, carrying my toolkit, all surplus parts being removed for racing, then put back afterwards for the journey home. Yet I cannot recall its ever letting me down. In those days, of course, only the very rich or the trade-supported could muster a van or a sidecar float as transport.

I never went out of my way to get involved with concours events, not that there were many at the time when I was most active. But I always started out with a clean and tidy machine that looked as though it was in general use. Even so, my much-modified KSS mentioned earlier managed to qualify for an award at a Velocette Owners Club event at Stanford Hall, much to my surprise. As for the hybrid vintage racer I described, this eventually turned up in the USA, having passed through several hands after I had sold it. It was re-restored to look like a standard road-going KSS and as such, won several concours awards in old bike exhibitions, though it still had the KTP cycle parts and presumably the crankcase with the KA engine number prefix! By British standards, it appeared to have been over-restored, judging from photographs I saw in an American magazine, and had suffered the ultimate indignity — the fitting of hand gearchange!

Being a long-standing member of the Vintage MCC has helped me in at least two respects. It has provided access to spares and information through contact with fellow members, and access to the Club Library and the earlier Marque Specialist until I took over this role about 12 years ago. It also enabled me to take part in sporting events run by the Club and in many others to which the Club had an invitation. For a while I belonged to the Velocette Owners Club too, until I packed in my job as Travelling Marshal with BEMSEE and foolishly sold my much-modified KSS.

It is always difficult to name specialists who have proved particularly helpful, as there have been so many and there is always risk of unintentionally missing someone out. But I would in particular like to mention Geoff Dodkin, who always seems to come up with what I need, apart from providing a wealth of good advice based on a lifetime of practical experience. I sometimes wonder whether the level of interest in the marque would be anything like so high if it were not for Geoff's infectious enthusiasm. In the early days, it was the late Arthur Lavington who kept me mobile, as did frequent visits to L. Stevens Ltd in Goldhawk Road, Shepherds Bush, and Roy Smith Motors, at that time in Kingston but now in New Malden. Today, it is a question of finding ohc parts wherever you can, as they are not often seen, even at autojumbles.

The enjoyment I have gained from riding and racing KSS models of various kinds must by now be obvious, although ironically I do not own one at present. I am fortunate enough to have graduated to the ownership of a genuine 1930 KTT, which has a fully authenticated Brooklands racing history and is still in full race trim. The only advice I can give to a prospective KSS owner is to take the plunge and buy the machine if one happens to come your way. It is a move that will never be regretted, for you will then own one of the world's greatest and most respected motorcycles.

Over the years I have got to know a great many Velocette enthusiasts, and one of those that I have known is Ken Blake, whom I first met in the early 1950s when he was racing a Mark IV KTT on the grass. In those days, Ken was working for the late George Goodall, who had a motorcycle shop in Epsom, but today Ken has his own business, Etna Motorcycles, in Parkstone, Dorset. One of his more recent acquisitions was an iron engine KSS, which he saved from ultimate dilapidation and fully restored, as can be seen from some of the photographs in this book. Ken was an obvious choice for interview, and the following are his comments:

JRC. Why are you so interested in the Velocette KSS?
KRB. I've always had a liking for them ever since riding my KTT on the grass thirty years ago.
JRC. What condition was your machine in when you found it, and were the faults you found common to the design?
KRB. It was in a very rough condition when found — a typical

Super Profile

'under the hedge' type of discovery. There is certainly nothing wrong with the design of any of the major parts.

JRC. What repair/renovation work has been done? Would there have been a better way of tackling the problem as, for example, the purchase of a machine in a better or worse condition?

KRB. The machine needed to be stripped and completely rebuilt. It had been well and truly butchered before it was finally abandoned. Most old Velocettes are found in this condition; those that have been restored seldom change hands.

JRC. Have you experienced any difficulty in obtaining parts? If so, what solutions did you find?

KRB. Fortunately, people seem to hang on to Velocette parts. After the usual hunt around, I found just what I wanted.

JRC. What kind of performance and handling does the machine have?

KRB. It handles very well, even though it hops about a bit on bumpy roads, due to its short wheelbase. I don't yet know its top speed for it has covered only 197 miles since its rebuild. But it will now cruise quite nicely at 60mph.

JRC. Has your machine won any prizes in Concours or similar events?

KRB. No. It was my intention to use the machine rather than prop it up on display.

JRC. Do you belong to an owner's club or clubs?

KRB. I am a member of the Vintage MCC, which I consider sufficient.

JRC. Is there a specialist you have found particularly helpful?

KRB. Yes, but you may be too modest to let me provide a name!

JRC. How would you sum up the enjoyment you get from your Velocette KSS?

KRB. The machine has the vintage look about it, but is able to do anything a post-vintage or post-war motorcycle can do.

JRC. What advice wuld you give to potential owners of a Velocette KSS?

KRB. Make sure you have all the bits before starting a rebuild. Also modify the rear drain pipe from the cambox to feed into the front drain pipe which enters the crankcase via a flap valve. The arrangement will appear similar to that of the later alloy engine, but will stop nearly all the oil leaks. It is also worth fitting a K17/5 cam.

The other machine featured in this book is a later, alloy engine model owned by Pat Manley, of Leigh, Dorset. Pat has tended to specialise in Velocettes, having restored in addition to this machine, a pre-war GTP two-stroke and a post-war MAC. His views on the later model are as follows:

JRC. Why are you so interested in the Velocette KSS?

PM. I have always been keen on Velocettes and wanted to own a pre-war 'top of the range' model for road use.

JRC. What condition was your machine in when you found it and were the faults common to the design?

PM. It was found dismantled, with some parts missing. I do not know of any faults in the basic design.

JRC. What repair/renovation work has been done? Would there have been a better way of tackling the problem as, for example, the purchase of a machine in better or worse condition?

PM. The machine required complete restoration. Fortunately, most of the missing parts were interchangeable with those from other Velocette models. Either approach to purchase will have its problems.

JRC. Have you experienced any difficulty in obtaining parts?

PM. New parts were obtained from Roy Smith Motors, and also from autojumbles and friends. Other, difficult to find parts, were made locally.

JRC. What kind of performance does the machine have?

PM. The performance is very good for a machine of its age, and the steering and braking are first class.

JRC. Has your machine won any prizes in concours or similar events?

PM. Yes, it has qualified for two concours awards.

JRC. Do you belong to an owners' club or clubs?

PM. The Velocette Owners Club which, although not well represented locally, brings Velocette owners together and has a good magazine.

JRC. Is there a specialist you have found particularly helpful?

PM. This is difficult to answer, as the necessity has never really arisen.

JRC. How would you sum up the enjoyment you get from your Velocette KSS?

PM. That's easy to answer. It is delightful to ride, and easy to maintain — who could ask for more?

Summing up, it is obvious that like all other thoroughbred machines, the Velocette KSS has its staunch devotees who consider it to be one of the best British designs, even though it has not been made since 1948 and even then was a continuation of what first saw the light of day as far back as 1925. Opinions vary as to whether the iron engine or the alloy engine versions are the most desirable to own, the former undoubtedly being the quicker, but at the disadvantage of being difficult to keep oiltight. The sad fact remains that, irrespective of the year of manufacture, the overhead camshaft Velocette is now becoming both difficult to find and expensive to acquire. These facts alone can be taken as pointers to the high regard in which these models are held.

Super Profile

BUYING

Buying any overhead camshaft Velocette is likely to prove a somewhat expensive proposition, irrespective of whether the machine is complete and running, or the classic box of bits and pieces 'awaiting restoration'. Overhead camshaft models of any make have always tended to demand high prices, as they are regarded as the 'thoroughbreds' of the classic bike world. And the Velocette is certainly no exception in this respect.

Only too often, machines that come up for sale are associated with some famous rider's name, with a price ticket that reflects this. So the first rule is to make sure there is adequate documentary evidence to support the claim and that the machine is the one referred to in the documentation. The next step is to verify the year of manufacture of the machine by reference to the engine and frame numbers. Of the two, the engine number is the more important from the reference viewpoint, because Veloce Limited based their service records on engine numbers arranged in numerical sequence. The frame numbers were not allocated in a similar sequence, so in consequence frame numbers are much more difficult to trace when this information alone is all that is presented. Fortunately, the original factory service records have survived, and are now in private hands. Always meticulously kept, they list engine, frame and gearbox numbers, the date the machine left the factory, and the name of the dealer who took delivery. Sometimes, the name and address of the first owner is available too.

A secondary source of information is the Vintage MCC's Machine Register, which is available to members. This lists similar information to that given in the factory records but, of course, relates only to members' machines that have been dated correctly and entered on the Register. There is sufficient information on record to allow any newly-found or newly-acquired machine to be dated with reasonable accuracy.

Sadly, a seemingly correct engine and frame number do not necessarily guarantee the specification of the machine will be as it appears. A high degree of interchange amongst Velocette parts makes it relatively easy for a machine to be 'updated' by the use of more modern parts, although in the main this relates to the earlier, iron engine models. It should be remembered that it was often the practice of older riders to adopt this technique, rather than keep changing machines as the later versions became available. It takes an expert to check machine detail in these circumstances; for example, it requires a very critical eye to differentiate between a 1930 KSS and one made a year later, yet one is a genuine vintage machine, according to the VMCC's definition, whereas the other is not. It is here, of course, that the advice of the Club Marque Specialist becomes most valuable.

Buying a machine that is completely dismantled will prove a much cheaper proposition than buying one complete that is a runner. But it is questionable whether this approach is advisable in the first instance. Invariably, some parts will be missing and others badly worn, such that they may possibly be beyond reclaiming. The chances of finding missing or replacement parts are now very slim indeed, so it could take a very long time to get the machine complete and back on to the road. Unfortunately, parts from the push-rod 'M' series models will prove of little help, so it is as well to recognise this problem right from the start.

When buying an early model (iron engine), points to look out for are a broken cambox casting with its obvious oil leaks, or a high degree of mechanical noise accompanied by sluggish performance. A drop in oil pressure, or low oil pressure, will allow the cambox to run dry, with disastrous results as far as the cams and rocker skids are concerned. Having twin front down tubes, the front half of the frame is unlikely to give trouble, but look for any cracks or brazed-up joints immediately behind the channel casting to which the three-or early four-speed gearbox is bolted. It is here that fractures are likely to occur. The lugs are not tapered which gives rise to stress points where the chainstay tubes enter. Check frame alignment too; it is relatively easy to put one of these frames out of line as the result of an accident or by attaching a heavy sidecar.

All the usual engine checks apply, with regard to compression, blue smoke from the exhaust, etc. If the bevels are meshed correctly, there should be a slight whine from them when the engine is cold, which will disappear as the engine warms up.

Much the same advice applies to the later, alloy engine models, as far as the engine is concerned. The frame is much more robust, and therefore unlikely to give rise to any problems. In the rare event of the machine having Dowty telescopic front forks, do make sure they hold air when they are correctly inflated. Seals are now impossible to obtain, and it does not take much of a leak to cause the forks to deflate and render the machine immobile (they

Super Profile

have no internal springs). Velocette telescopic forks can be fitted with ease, in their place, but this modification will, of course, destroy the original specification of the machine.

Little has been said about the gearbox, early or late type. Most gearbox problems are caused by allowing the oil level to fall too low, which accelerates wear and leads to the ultimate failure of the bearings or some vital part. It is also important to recognise that rainwater can leak into the gearbox via the external clutch operating cable, emulsifying the oil and causing premature bearing failure. It is always wise to check the gearbox oil, as this will give a good indication of how the machine has been maintained.

The Velocette clutch requires a special understanding, as it operates like no other motorcycle clutch and needs a very special adjustment routine that has to be followed to the letter. Exasperation with the clutch has led to many a Velocette being sold, yet if the owner had only taken the care to set it up and adjust it according to the manufacturer's recommendations, there would have been no problem at all.

Perhaps the most frequently mentioned problem of all is the tendency for the crankcase to fill with oil when the machine is left standing for a while, sometimes to the extent that the oil tank empties of its content completely and oil floods into the primary chaincase and out on to the floor. This happens when there is a small amount of wear in the gear-type oil pump, located within the right-hand crankcase, or if the spring-loaded ball valve in the right-hand end of the hollow mainshaft is not seating correctly. Little can be done with regard to the oil pump, as it is a tricky task to withdraw it without damage and rub down the machined facing of the pump housing to take up the end float of the gear pinions. Far simpler to fit a tap in the main oil feed, making sure it is of at least equal bore size to that of the main feed pipe. But there is a snag – any failure to turn the tap on when using the machine will result in a totally wrecked engine. Veloce Limited tried the tap idea on some of their early models, but it was soon withdrawn as the result of warranty claims for seized engines; owners could not remember to turn it on! The ball valve in the hollow mainshaft is easily re-seated by unscrewing the left-hand thread nut, placing the ball on its seating within, and giving it a smart tap with a thin drift and hammer, after both nut and ball have been cleaned off with petrol. Particular emphasis is made of this oil problem, as it is quite common, and easily dealt with, but may nonetheless give the impression that something is fundamentally wrong with the machine that is for sale.

Above all else, do not pay a high price for a machine that has poor handling characteristics, inefficient braking, or sluggish performance. All these faults indicate that something could be seriously wrong with the machine, which will necessitate immediate, and possibly expensive, remedial action. If you buy under these circumstances, make sure the price paid reflects this need for attention.

Super Profile

CLUBS, SPECIALISTS & BOOKS

Clubs

The club that caters most for those who own an overhead camshaft model is obviously the **Velocette Owners Club**, which has its own spares scheme in the form of a separate, limited company. Open Days are held regularly at the spares headquarters in Huncote, Leicestershire, and membership of the Club is necessary to take advantage of this service. The Club also has its own magazine, entitled appropriately *Fishtail*. Further information about the Club and membership is available from: Ted Broadbridge, c/o The Velocette Owners Club, The Old Chapel, Cheney End, Huncote, Leicestershire, LE9 6AD.

It is also worth while giving consideration to membership of the **Vintage Motor Cycle Club**, despite this club's relatively high annual subscription. Having joined this club, which has a total world-wide membership of more than 5,000, access then becomes available to the Club's Library, where searches can be carried out for a nominal sum and, if required, photocopies of the relevant documents supplied at an economic page rate. Membership also permits use of the voluntary services of the Club's marque specialists which, in the case of Velocette, happens to be the author of this book! Enquiries about membership of the VMCC should be made to:
Jim Hammant, Red Oaks, Mill Road, Lower Shiplake, Henley-on-Thames, Oxon, RG9 3LN.

Specialists

With the demise of the British motorcycle industry, those who specialised exclusively in the Velocette marque needed to take on other agencies in order to survive, the more so when their stock of spare parts began to run down and could not be replaced. A few disappeared altogether, but of those that have survived, most can offer help in some way or other, even if it is limited to supplying just one or two parts off a very long list of requirements. In consequence, it is often a case of looking up the names and addresses of these specialists in the classic motorcycle magazines and shopping around, getting a part here, and a part there.

My personal experience in dealing with the specialists during recent years is limited to the south of England, and in this context I can strongly recommend two who will also undertake repair work with real competence. The third concern specialises only in spares, to the best of my belief:

Geoff Dodkin, 346, Upper Richmond Road West, East Sheen, London, SW14 7JS. Phone: 01 876 8779

R.F. Seymour Ltd, Hawthorn Works, Park Street, Thame, Oxfordshire, OX9 3HT. Phone: 084 421 2277

Roy Smith Motors, 116-124, Burlington Road, New Malden, Surrey. Phone: 01 949 6909/5731

These addresses and telephone numbers were correct at the time of going to press, but should always be checked prior to making contact.

Books

Although this is the first book to be devoted exclusively to the ohc KSS models, a complete chapter on the Model K and its successors will be found in the book **Always in the Picture** by the late Bob Burgess and the Author, which was first published in 1971. A revised and enlarged edition first published in 1980, is currently available under the Haynes/Foulis imprint.

The ohc KSS models are also covered in some detail in two out-of-print books which are occasionally found at autojumbles and book sales. They are:
The Book of the Velocette, original edition by Leslie K. Heathcote, and later edition by Ferrers Leigh, both editions published by Pitman, and **Velocette** by R.W. Burgess, one of the Motor Cycle Maintenance and Repair Series of books published by C. Arthur Pearson.

The manufacturer's original **Instruction Book** and **Spare Parts List** for both the iron engine and alloy engine KSS models can sometimes be found at autojumbles too, these books being comprehensive, particularly in the case of the alloy engine models, and the spares lists fully illustrated. A portion from the original instruction book relating to the engine of the later, post-1935 models, will be found in the appendices to the book **Always in the Picture** together with the wiring diagrams for these models. **Bruce Main-Smith Retail Ltd,** of P.O. Box 20, Leatherhead, Surrey, can often supply good quality xerox copies of original Instruction Books and Spare Parts Lists, and is certainly worth contacting (0372 375615). He can also supply printed facsimiles of the original Instruction Book and Spare Parts List for the 1925-31 ohc models.

25

Super Profile

PHOTO GALLERY

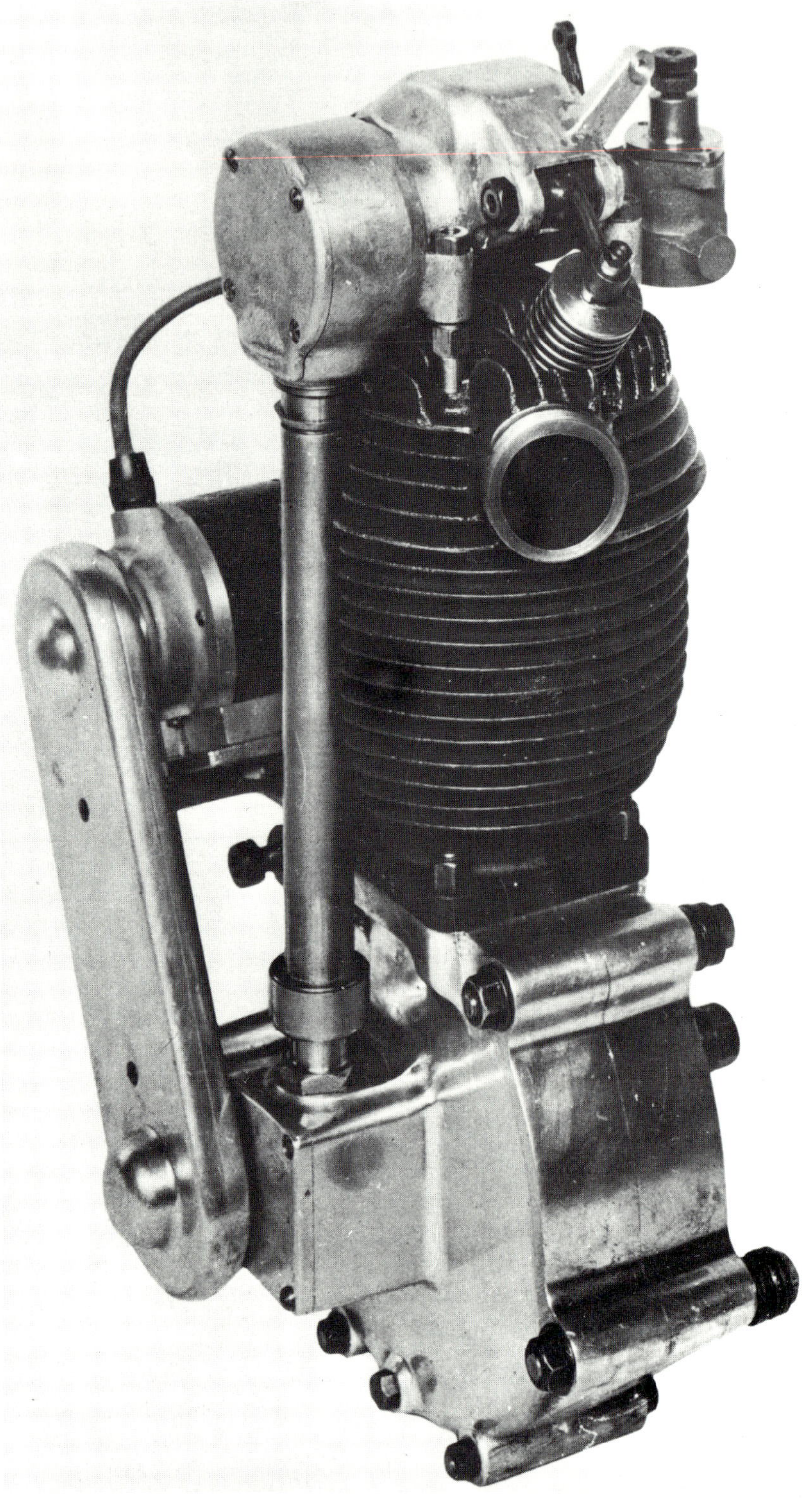

1. Percy Goodman, the originator of the overhead camshaft Velocette. This photograph was taken shortly before his death in 1953.

2. The prototype overhead camshaft engine of 1924. Note the oil pump attached to the left-hand end of the cambox and the long, slender vertical coupling drive up the right-hand side of the cylinder.

Super Profile

3. A complete prototype machine of 1924. A Druid front fork is fitted, and the petrol tank has a separate compartment for oil, the lubrication system working on the 'total loss' principle. Only three of these prototypes were made.

4. The 1926 Model KT, which sold for £65. Designed with touring work in mind, this model had footboards fitted. Later models were fitted with a Webb front fork, not the Druids as shown here.

5. Do any of these models still exist? This is the somewhat cheaper Model KE of 1926, which retailed at £58. The most distinguishing feature is the use of a Brampton front fork.

3

4

5

Super Profile

6. This machine was used successfully by Freddie Hicks in 1928 for record breaking attempts at Brooklands and other high speed venues. It is, in fact, an early KTT model, as shown by the webbed crankcase and strutted Webb front fork.

7. An artist's impression of the 1930 KSS model, fitted with Miller electric lighting equipment. It was most probably drawn for use in the 1930 catalogue.

Super Profile

8.

9.

8. All of the iron engine models used a light grade of Webb front fork with parallel-sided tubes, and twin friction dampers.

9. This engine number is indicative of the late vintage period, although it is used for a 1934 model. The original crankcases were damaged beyond repair.

10. Possibly the most handsome of all the iron engine models, due to the effect of the large capacity petrol tank. In some respects, the KSS model was years ahead of its time.

11. The vital regulating screw that controls the oil pressure in the lubrication system. Its setting is very sensitive once near the recommended 8-10psi when the engine is warm.

10.

11.

29

Super Profile

12. The owner has found that if these two oil drain pipes are united, a much more oil-tight engine results. The drain is to the crankcase, via the one-way valve.

13. The post-vintage cambox has a rounded bottom to the end cover and only four retaining screws. Note the small but essential drain pipe to the inlet valve guide.

14. The big, 8 inch diameter Miller headlamp, is another typical Velocette fitting. It has a three-point mounting on the front fork.

15. Another typical Velocette fitting, the very efficient 'fishtail' silencer that gives the machine its characteristic exhaust note. This is a 'pattern' and not an original, which may result in loss of performance.

Super Profile

16. All Velocette chaincases tend to leak oil, but the early type with screws around its periphery is much better than the later 'band' type.

17. The transfer says it all. The Velocette clutch has a very special adjustment technique that needs to be followed to the letter. To try and adjust it by other means is to court disaster.

31

Super Profile

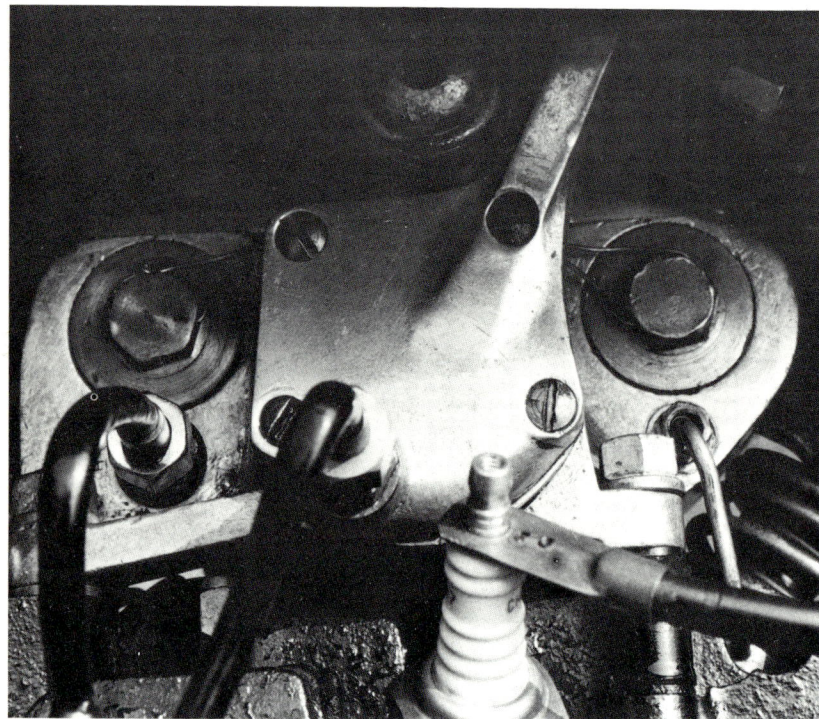

18. This tank transfer was used from 1930 to the end of the 1936 season, yet the factory did not win another TT during this period!

19. The rocker pins need to be wired together, otherwise they will come unscrewed and render the engine immobile.

20. An essential modification – the fitting of a tap in the main oil feed line to prevent oil draining into the crankcase whilst the machine is standing. But one must remember to turn it on!

Super Profile

21. A small size of the standard petrol tank transfer is used for the rear mudguard.

22. The front brake has a built-in water deflector which proves quite effective. Note the speedometer drive taken from the inside of the brake drum.

23. A useful fitment not seen today – a front mudguard stay that doubles as a front wheel stand, to make wheel removal easier.

Super Profile

24.

25.

24. A special peg spanner is needed to slacken and retighten this exhaust pipe union nut. It can be wired to the cylinder head steady to prevent it from unscrewing.

25. The rear number plate, with a type of rear light that is no longer legal. The area of lens is too small.

26. An Amal Type 6 carburetter is fitted as standard. The flame trap is not a standard fitting – more usually found on the KTP models.

26.

Super Profile

27. The rear chain adjuster and the unusual torque bolt fixing for the rear brake plate.

28. The cover for the belt that drives the dynamo from the engine pulley. The transfer is that for the headstock, not usually found here.

29. The rear brake has a built-in water deflector too. The strengthening plate between the rear wheel spindle and the brake operating shaft is missing.

Super Profile

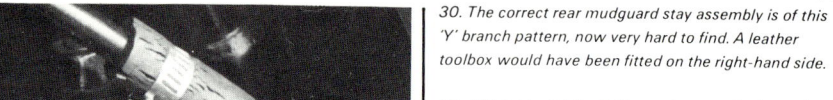

30. The correct rear mudguard stay assembly is of this 'Y' branch pattern, now very hard to find. A leather toolbox would have been fitted on the right-hand side.

31. Although of John Bull manufacture, the kneegrips were manufactured to the company's own design.

32. The late-type four-speed gearbox has its positive stop mechanism contained internally and has the later type of kickstart ratchet assembly. It is suspended by two studs from the channel behind the engine.

33. The front-mounted Miller dynamo is of the three brush type, with no separate provision for voltage control.

Super Profile

34. This BTH 'square type' magneto is a somewhat unusual fitting as, when a magneto of this shape was used, it was normally of ML manufacture.

35. The cylinder head steady is an essential fitting, if the machine is to run smoothly without vibration.

36. The steering head transfer in its correct location. Known amongst Velocette enthusiasts as the 'naughty lady' transfer!

Super Profile

37. This is the post-war type of oil tank transfer, used only because the original, much simpler, transfer is now very difficult to obtain. Many early KSS owners prefer to run their machines on a vegetable-base oil such as Castrol 'R'.

38. A retouched 'works' photograph of the 1938 alloy engine KSS model, used in the 1938 catalogue.

39. An unusual location for the frame number on the later models. It is stamped on the upper of the two front down tube lugs, on the right-hand side.

Super Profile

40. Yet another pattern silencer, though of the correct profile. The original silencer had more holes in the fishtail, a wider opening in the exit and, unseen, a much more efficient internal baffle arrangement of the louvred type.

41. It is not generally known that even models built to the touring KTS model specification had an engine with a KSS engine number prefix.

42. The plain area of the right-hand crankcase immediately below the lower bevel housing shows this to be a pre-1939 engine. From 1939 onwards, a crankcase suction filter was added, with its attendant bulge.

39

Super Profile

43. The familiar 'D' shape toolbox, characteristic of the late thirties Velocette models and continued post-war.

44. A close-up of the Type 6 Amal carburetter with its angled floatchamber. A shallow bellmouth is the correct fitting. Note the 'easy starting' device which enables the throttle to be held at a constant setting whilst starting.

45. The extra-long bolt extending from the gearbox end cover is the oil level plug. Oil filler is on the left.

Super Profile

46. In general construction the later four-speed gearbox is very similar to the early four-speed type with internal footchange mechanism. But the method of mounting is entirely different and the external linkage on the left.

47. Of the two-brush DVR type, the Miller dynamo has its carbon pile voltage regulator mounted separately, but immediately above it.

48. Following racing practice, the oil tank has a built-in froth tower to prevent excess oil loss. The transfer is correct, but the varnish has hardened, making it translucent.

Velocette

41

Super Profile

49. The vent from the froth tower is used to advantage to lubricate the final drive chain.

50. The 'Y' pipe from the cambox is an all alloy engine KSS recognition feature. The spark plug is of the 14mm, long reach type.

51. The lower end of the 'Y' pipe drains into the crankcase without need for the one-way valve used on the early models. The system contains a 'conical hat' built-in filter to obviate the risk of debris reaching the oil pump.

Super Profile

52.

53.

54.

52. The rear wheel is of the quickly detachable type, the brake drum and sprocket being retained to the hub by three nuts. Spindle is of the knock out type.

53. The Velocette method of clutch adjustment never changed; it relied upon a peg passed through holes in the final drive sprocket to rotate the spring carrier.

54. A BTH magneto with cable-operated ignition advance was the standard fitting. It was a good, reliable magneto that gave very little trouble in service.

43

Super Profile

55. Unlike the early models, the magneto did not have a platform-type base mounting. It is held to the inner drive casing by three nuts, which can prove quite difficult to remove.

56. A close-up of the short but very sturdy prop stand. It will hold the machine quite firmly on most hard surfaces.

57. Although a rear stand is fitted, it has to be unbolted before it can be used and is not of the usual spring-up type. The rearmost end of the mudguard is detachable to make rear wheel removal easy.

58. The use of a front wheel stand continued, in order to aid removal of the front wheel. But the machine needed to be supported on the rear stand first, to make it secure.

59. The front brake drum has the characteristic Velocette water deflector and the curved brake operating arm favoured in later years. The short cross-brace between the fork tubes forms the peg for the torque plate location.

60. The use of the knee grips made to pattern by John Bull continued on the alloy engine models ...

Super Profile

61. ... as did the 8 inch diameter Miller headlamp. Despite its size, it never provided a particularly good light for high speed riding at night.

62. This type of fork friction damper was used until the end of the 1938 season. The 1939 and later model had the adjuster in the form of a moulded, circular knob, like that found on old domestic radiators.

63. Velocette were not shy in having their name displayed on various component parts!

Super Profile

64. The heavy side valance on the left-hand side of the rear mudguard helped keep road filth off the chain. It was dished inwards, to clear the secondary chainguard.

65. The cover over the flat belt drive to the dynamo is of more pleasing shape on the later models.

66. A close-up of the plug that needs to be removed for an oil pressure gauge to be connected when the oil pressure is checked. Low oil pressure will quickly wreck the top end of the engine.

Velocette

64

65

66

47

Super Profile

67. The author at Brands Hatch in 1955, riding the 'hybrid' vintage KSS racer referred to in the text.

68. Another photograph of the author, taken much later, during a very cold road race meeting at Snetterton. This is the much modified 1938 KSS model mentioned in the text, nearing its final stages of modernisation.

Super Profile

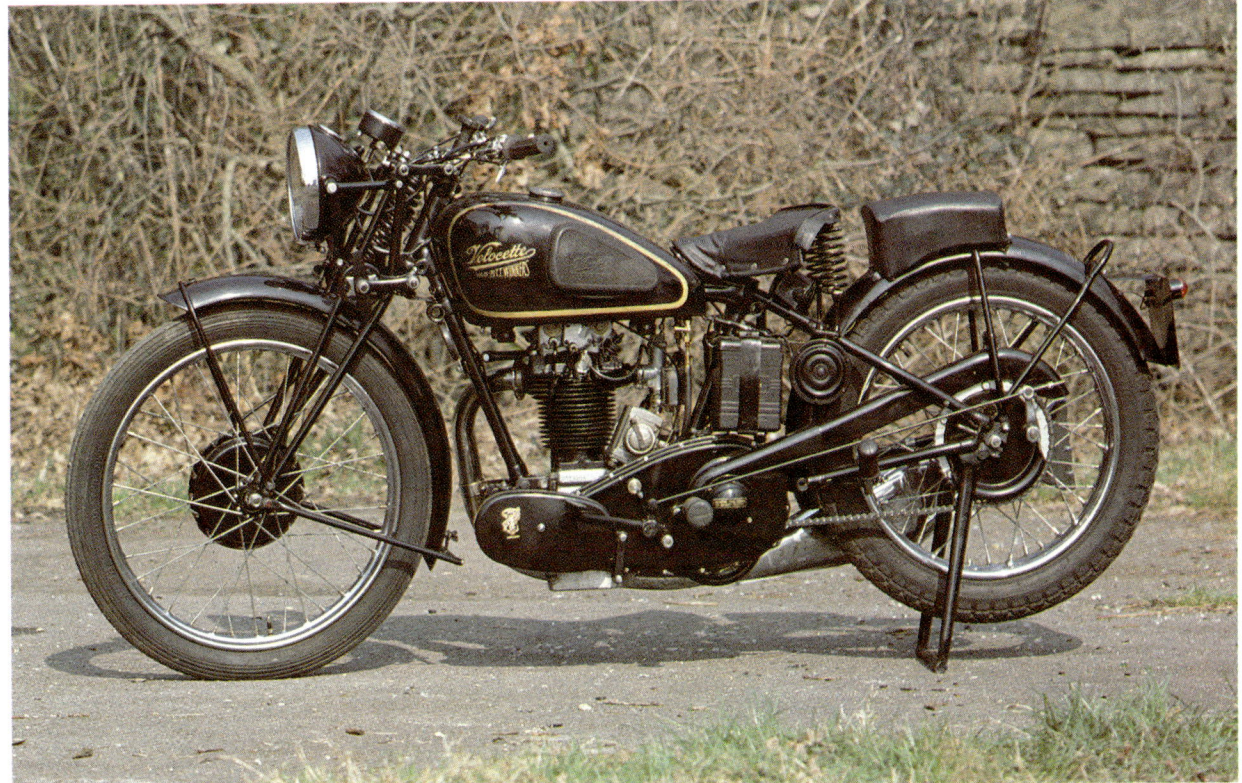

C1. Judged by any standards, the 1934 KSS model is a very handsome machine when compared with most of its contemporaries.

C2. It is difficult to imagine that this machine has been rebuilt from a discarded, rusty wreck, by Ken Blake of Etna Motorcycles, Parkstone, Dorset.

Super Profile

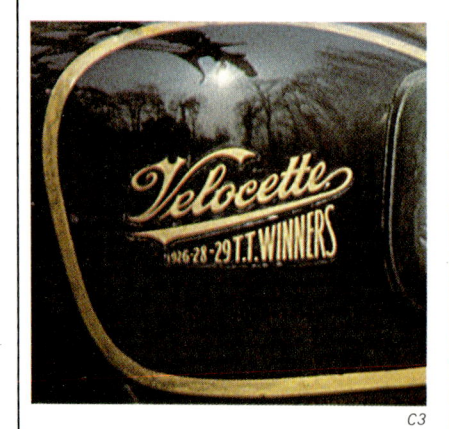

C3. At one time the 'TT Winners' transfer was almost impossible to obtain. Thanks to the VMCC Transfer Scheme, exact replicas were made and are now readily available.

C4. The deep, larger capacity petrol tank did much to enhance the appearance of the later iron engine models, being of a particularly pleasant shape.

C5. The petrol tank does not have quite the capacity one might expect. A large area on the underside is hollowed out to provide clearance for the cambox.

Super Profile

C6. The case for the magneto drive chain is of simple design, with a cast-in Velocette motif. It is secured by just two screws. Note the clean lines of the vertical shaft drive to the overhead camshaft.

C7. The early-pattern Webb front fork has twin side dampers and has lighter gauge tubing than that of later designs. The handling characteristics are very good.

C8. The alloy engine KSS made during the late thirties has a quite different appearance, more in keeping with the times. Not many parts can be interchanged between the early and late models, with the exception of some engine components.

Super Profile

C9. This 1938 model, owned by Pat Manley of Leigh, Dorset, has been carefully rebuilt to as near original specification as possible. It has proved very reliable and is a pleasure to ride, even by modern standards.

C10. Until the girder front fork ceased to be made, Veloce Limited took the speedometer drive from the front wheel via a pinion on the end of the front wheel hub, within the brake drum.

Super Profile

C11. The "TT Winners' petrol tank transfer was discontinued after the end of the 1936 season. One sees the simpler transfer mounted at all angles, but this one is about right.

C12. The gold tank lining is seen in a variety of widths and outlines after restorations have been completed. The width is about right in this photograph, but the outline is just a little too rounded.

C13. The petrol tank of the alloy engine model has a large underside cutaway too, to give clearance to the even larger cambox-cum-cylinder head.

Super Profile

C14. The case for the magneto drive chain is secured by nine screws on the later models, the back portion being integral with the cover of the lower bevel housing.

C15. The alloy engine models have an Amal downdraught carburetter, fitted with an 'easy starting' device in the form of a hand adjustable throttle stop.

Super Profile

C16

C17

C18

C16. There is a striking difference in appearance between the alloy and the iron cylinder heads. Although still forward mounted, the dynamo is positioned much higher and a different shape of drive belt cover is fitted.

C17. There is a blanking plug in the cambox cover to permit checking of the oil pressure by means of a gauge. The vertical shaft cover is of similar appearance to that used for the earlier iron engine models but differs in length.

C18. A useful fitment is the short but sturdy prop stand, which aids secure, roadside parking. The rear stand is less easy to use, requiring a spanner to unbolt it prior to use.

55

Super Profile

C19. The KSS model has a 21 inch diameter front wheel and a 20 inch diameter rear wheel, which helps to distinguish it from the almost identical KTS model which has 19 inch diameter wheels and heavier mudguards.

C20. A colourful display of pre-war Velocette catalogues. The front cover of these catalogues often featured the overhead camshaft models, always regarded as the top of the range.